ession

intercession

CESAR CASTELLANOS D.

SEMINAR

LEVEL 2

TEACHERS' GUIDE

interc

# EDITORIAL TEAM

CESAR CASTELLANOS D. © 2003
Published by G12 Editors
sales@g12bookstore.com

ISBN 1-932285-30-X

Made in Colombia

Printed in Colombia

# CONTENTS

Forward

# CONTENTS

The material you now hold in your hands was birthed from our own experience within the church through the leaders that we developed over the years, in ministry. Even though we knew from the day our church opened in 1983, that we would be a cell church and would have an immense effect on our city, it was not until sometime in1990 that the Lord removed the veil to expose to us, the vision of the government of twelve. In the wake of this revelation, the church experienced a growth explosion that has superceded all records on church growth with no waning in sight. Along with the excitement of growth, as pastors we were challenged to develop these new believers that the Lord entrusted to us.

During this time God gave me a Rhema word for our ministry: "I will give you the ability to quickly train people." This was a word we truly needed because up until then, it was taking at least two years to train a cell leader. The demand was great and the process was just too long. But after that word, the heavens opened up and a special anointing was released upon each person that was helping us in the ministry. Now, the entire congregation, from the least to the greatest, reeled with motivation; they wanted to be a part of the vision. The mind of the people, even ours, was powerfully impressed with the vision of growth but the necessary components were not in place for the most advantageous operating system.

A formula has been developed and implemented as a result of the word the Lord gave, thanks to the team of pastors and leaders that Jesus gave us.  How would we actually train faster? What tools would be used? The best possible method was being created for our use according to the results we saw as we went along.  We then decided to put them into motion as a part of our vision.

For many years prior, we did not want to be away from the church because we felt that our vision was still being established. Neither did we want to teach about church growth, until we had a congregation to back it up. Now that God has allowed us to become one of the largest churches in the world, with an average of 25,000 leadership school students, we can only thank God for His mercy to our country and for having lifted up our church as the leader of that great spiritual awakening which has been able to influence the nations of the earth. It is our prayer that this material blesses your life, your church and your ministry. May each one of you fulfill God's purpose in your lives.

In the love of Christ,

Cesar and Claudia Castellanos.

# Moving the Hand of God Through Intercession

1

## TEACHING OBJECTIVE

The student will understand the meaning of intercession, its importance to the ministry and the purpose behind each biblical teaching.

## STUDENT OBJECTIVE

1 The student will define the word "intercession"

2 The student will explain the things on which intercession depends on.

Jeremiah 33:3

CORRESPONDING
BIBLICAL
FOUNDATION

1 Samuel 1:9-18

Luke 18:1-8

Luke 6:12-13

John 17:9-24

Hebrews 2:14-15

Hebrews 5:1-10

Mark 2:3-12

Matthew 18:19-20

John 7:1-10

Genesis 18:17-33

Ezekiel 22:30

I Kings 18:30-40

1 Samuel 7:8-10

2 Chronicles 20:5-12

Daniel 9:15-18

KEY VERSE

"And pray in the Spirit on all
occasions with all kinds of prayers
and requests. With this in mind, be
alert and always keep on praying for
all the saints"
**(Ephesians 6:18)**

## A. DEFINITION

Intercession is the act of bringing one or more requests before God and the requests are usually for the sake of other people. The term comes from the Hebrew verb "paga" and the Greek "Entygjano," both mean "to meet someone" The significance is "seeking help."

## B. INTERCESSION DEPENDES ON TWO THINGS

1.    A sense of solidarity which produces a desire for others to be blessed.

2.    The intercessor's conviction that God is able to save or bless the person for whom intercession is being made.

## C. MOVING THE HAND OF GOD THROUGH INTERCESSION

"Call out to me and I will respond and will show you great and hidden things that you do not know" (Jeremiah 33:3).

Throughout history, human beings have had to go through all types of difficulties. In these adversities, however, they discovered the secret of intercession and learned how to cause God to move His hand on their behalf.

Hannah, Samuel's mother, interceded until she received what she asked for (1 Samuel 1:9-18).

The troubled widow who persevered (Luke 18:1-8) received favor from an unjust judge. If this took place with an unjust man, how much more favor might we receive from our God who is merciful?

## D. WHY INTERCEDE?

History is full of examples that should motivate us to incorporate intercession into our lives as we seek to conquer situations for Christ.

We should intercede for many reasons:

- To confirm a team of twelve apostles (Luke 6:12-13).
- To meet the needs of the group of twelve (John 17:9).
- To receive protection from evil (John 17:15).
- To be sanctified (John 17:17).
- To build and maintain unity (John 17:21).
- To elevate disciples to the same ministerial level as their mentors (John 17:24).

## E. THE NATURE OF AN INTERCESOR

Jesus exemplified what an intercessor should be. He served time into our humanity and came to destroy the one who holds the power of death; the devil. Jesus came to free all from the enslavement of the fear of death.
(Hebrews 2:14-15).

Scripture describes what an intercessor should be (Hebrews 4:15)

- A priestly ministry.
- Compassionate and merciful.
- Approved (after having been tempted in every way).
- Holy.

Hebrews 5:1-10

- They bring offerings and sacrifices (Hebrews 5:1).
- They are patient with those who are ignorant and lost (Hebrews 5:2).
- They lean on God though surrounded by weakness (Hebrews 5:2).
- They pray for themselves and for others (Hebrews 5:3).

- They offer up prayers and supplications, crying and tears and they are heard because they pray with respect (Hebrews 5:7).
- They are obedient to God (Hebrews 5:8).
- They know that intercession is the way to perfection and accept the responsibility to shape salvation for those who obey the Word (Hebrews 5:9).
- If they are faithful, God will honor them by placing them in an apostolic ministry (Hebrews 5:10).

## F. SPECIFIC INTERCESSORY PRAYERS

### 1. PRAYER TO HEAL PARALYSIS (MARK 2:3-12).

This story indicates the importance of being in one accord. The paralytic's four friends felt compassion for him and decided to open up the roof. Their action symbolizes opening up the heavens with our prayers and taking our needs to Jesus so that He may show mercy. (Matthew 18:19-20)

The paralysis in this story may represent either a life or a ministry that cannot stand on its own and needs the faith and the effort of intercessors to make the miracle happen.

### 2. PRAYER FOR THOSE WHO SUPPORT THE MINISTRY (Luke 7:1-10).

Although the centurion in this story was not a Jew, he had gained the appreciation of the elders of Israel for his generosity in constructing a synagogue. The elders saw his generous attitude as an argument in his favor. As leaders, it is your duty to go before God in favor of those who carry the financial weight of the ministry in which you participate.

### 3. PRAYER AGAINST JUDGMENT UPON THE RIGHTEOUS (Genesis 18:17-33).

Abraham interceded to save the lives of 10 righteous people in Sodom and Gomorrah but there were truly not even 10. Calculations place the average population of these two cities at

10,000 people, so the Lord essentially promised to spare the city if at least one righteous person could be found among each one thousand inhabitants. Sadly, there was not even one. If we, however discover intercession and pray vigilantly we can avert many judgments over our cities and nations. God seeks people to stand in the gap and have faith to defer judgments (Ezekiel 22:30).

## 4. PRAYER TO RECONCILE PEOPLE TO GOD (I Kings 18:30-40).

Elijah was a unique man. He was daring in all he did and his voice did not even tremble when he told the King of Israel that it would not rain again over that nation until he said so. That is indeed what actually happened. Elijah was a man who had the same passions as any other human being but the difference in his life was the type of faith that he had.

God allowed this drought to occur so that the people who had hardened their hearts and were far from Him would listen to every word that the prophet said. They had already lived through a drought that lasted 3 1/2 years and they were not willing to go through more of the same. For this reason, Elijah's life was an inspiration for them.

This passage establishes several important principles: 1 Kings 18

Vs. 30.    The power of convocation: Together the people drew near to Him and restored the altar of the Lord, which was in ruins.

Vs. 31.    The government of the twelve: The twelve stones represent twelve firm leaders in the work of God over which the weight of the ministry may rest.

Vs. 33.    The cross: The wood represents the cross of Christ.

Vs. 34.    The four steps needed to complete his mission: Many people know these steps as the four steps in the ladder of success: Win, consolidate, disciple and send.

Vs. 36-37. God's support in all of our efforts: Elijah showed us how to ask for this in prayer.

Vs. 38.    Revival: God's fire fell from the sky and consumed everything around it.

Vs. 39.    Group confession: Elijah lead all the people to confess
that the Lord is God.

## 5. PRAYER FOR PROTECTION FROM THE ENEMY
(I Samuel 7:8-10).

God accepted the prayer of his servant and the heavens
thundered on that very day. He struck fear into them and then
they were all conquered.

## 6. THE MIRACLE OF INTERCESSION
(2 Chronicles 20:5-12).

Jehoshaphat was between a rock and a hard place with no way
out. The most powerful and numerous armies had surrounded
his people and he knew that if God did not intervene that none of
them would live. God confronted them and said, "Be still and know
that I am God." The Lord can change the circumstances in one
instant. He seeks people who dare to believe Him and are able to
move His hand through intercession.

## 7. SUBSTITUTE PRAYER ON BEHALF OF A NATION
(Daniel 9:15-18).

Whether we like it or not, it is our duty as leaders to present ourselves before God on behalf of our people. Jehoshaphat
learned the secret to bringing down legions of angels which have
full power to transform circumstances in a positive way
(2 Chronicles 20:15-18).

## EVALUATION

Evaluate the class in order to find out to what degree are they
putting intercession into practice.
What was taught may also be evaluated in class.

It is important for students to do research on the biblical
characters that were used as examples of intercessors in the
class.

# RECOMMENDED METHODOLOGY

The question and answer method is an effective way to introduce the lesson and correct mistaken concepts that the students may have concerning intercession.

Lecturing is the best way to explain this lesson. Some type of project that links to the Evangelism Seminar is also recommended.

# APPLICATION

Throughout this week, apply all the concepts learned about intercession to your life.

# STUDENTS' ASSIGNMENT

The student should do a project concerning the areas in which our country needs intercession.

# 1 Questionnaire for further Study

1. What is intercession?

_____

_____

2. Intercession depends on what?

a._____

b._____

3. How can you move the hand of God through intercession?

_____

_____

4. Why intercession is so important for the church?

_____

_____

5. According to Hebrews 4:15, who should be intercessors?

_____

_____

6. According to Hebrews 5:1-10, what should intercessors do?

_____

_____

7. Which type of prayers should we use?

a._____

b._____

c._____

d._____

e._____

f._____

g._____

# Intercession Part 1

LESSON

## TEACHING OBJECTIVES

The student will understand that prayer is the key to fruitful ministry.

The student will understand that prayer enables leaders to take their ministries into dimensions that they have never imagined possible.

## STUDENT OBJECTIVES

1 The student will cite Bible verses that indicate which kinds of prayers produce fruit.

2 The student will explain how to obtain victory through prayer.

BIBLICAL FOUNDATIONAL
REFERENCE
Matthew 26:41

CORRESPONDING
BIBLICAL
FOUNDATION

Ephesians 1:4

Acts 1:14-15

Luke 11:1

Genesis 18:18

Deuteronomy 29:29

Acts 10:1-5

Matthew 9:37-38

Genesis 12:2

Psalm 2:8

2 Corinthians 10:4-5

Revelations 12: 11

KEY VERSE

"Pray continually"
**(1 Thessalonians 5:17)**

# A. PRAYERS THAT STRENGTHEN YOUR MINISTRY

God chose us before the foundation of the world (Ephesians 1:4), so we must understand that we are spiritual beings who live in earthly bodies. In His divine wisdom, God created the spirit first and then the body. The physical body's five senses should serve the spirit and yet we often act to the contrary. Just as the body needs physical nourishment, the spirit needs spiritual nourishment. We can only be nourished and strengthened spiritually according to the measure that we receive the Word of God and remain alert in prayer. God will restore His covenant with any person, family or nation that turns to Him in prayer. To such people, He has promised to be their God and to make them His holy people (Leviticus 26:12). There are several kinds of prayer that will help in that process.

1. Prayer that takes your disciples to Jesus (Acts 1:14-15).

Andrew gave us a model when he took Simon Peter to Jesus. Every leader should do the same thing in prayer. Take each of the twelve disciples that you are training to Jesus in prayer.

2. Prayer that teaches your disciples how to pray (Luke 11:1, Deuteronomy 29:29).

Prayer is a relationship in which you open your heart to God and in which He reveals His secrets to you. The best thing you can do for your disciples is to guide them into intimacy with God.

## 3. Prayer with a built-in blessing (Acts 10:1-5).

Cornelius prayed so effectively that he received multiple blessings:

- God sent an angel to speak to him.
- God sent someone from the "main 12 team" to go and preach to them.
- He had the privilege of hosting the first cell group meeting in his house.
- God used his home as the birthplace of the church.
- The Word of God and the Spirit of God united to bless all of the faithful ones in that meeting.
- They all entered into the covenant of baptism.

## 4. Prayer for the miraculous fish catch (Luke 5:4-11).

This kind of prayer should be used in conjunction with any evangelistic activity in which the Lord is expected to yield an abundant harvest of souls. In any ministry where the people desire to win souls, they must charge the atmosphere with a cloud of glory that can only be brought about through prayer and fasting. Reaching the lost is spiritual work. We must use the weapons that God has given us to ensure success.

## 5. Prayer for students in the school of leaders (Matthew 9:37-38).

A leader's success is measured by the number of people that the leader brings to the encounter meetings. If these people successfully go through the post-encounter, they will be able to go on to the school of leaders. The number of students in the school of leaders is an important indicator of how many cell groups will be developed in the coming year.

## 6. Prayer that claims a promise (Genesis 12:2, Psalm 2:8).

Any ministry starts with God burning into our hearts His desire to reach a specific group of people. The nation that God wants to give us must come from within us just as Isaac came from Abraham and Sarah, just as Jacob, came from Isaac and then the twelve tribes came from Jacob. God still works the same way today. To a leader his twelve disciples are like his spiritual children, from whom will come spiritual grandchildren, totaling one hundred and forty-four. Then our spiritual great-grandchildren come, totaling one thousand seven hundred and twenty-eight. Every leader should impart this promise to each disciple.

## B. HOW TO CLAIM VICTORY IN PRAYER

To do the work of God requires the use of spiritual weapons that He has made available.

1. Take the offensive in prayer
   (2 Corinthians 10:4-5).

The weapons of God are powerful and will help you do the following:

- Tear down arguments. Arguments are legal rights that the enemy holds in his hands; when we ignore them, he uses them against us. Through prayer, God reveals this deception and 99% of the battle is won. We win the remaining 1% when we use our faith to destroy those arguments on the cross.

- Tear down every pretension. That sets itself up against the knowledge of God. Through prayer, we can tear down every prideful spirit that tries to undermine the lordship of Jesus.

- Take every thought captive. One of the enemy's strategies is to plant deceitful thoughts in the minds of those who serve God to sap their strength to overcome.

2. Overcome the enemy (Revelations 12:11).

Three things will help you succeed:

> A. The power of the blood of the Lamb. Not only does the blood of Jesus cleanse us from sin but is also a weapon of warfare to go against the forces of evil.
> B. The word of your testimony. There should be a strong connection between what you confess. Our deeds should

follow our words.

C. Willingness to sacrifice. Jesus said that he who does not despise his own life cannot be His disciple.

## CONCLUSION

You already have in your hand the master key that will open all kinds of doors. Use it effectively, in each stage of your ministry's development.

## EVALUATION

The teacher can evaluate if the students' objectives that were taught in this lesson were achieved (part by using questions and answers and part by the homework). If the students are working on a ministry project, this important tool will be especially useful.

## RECOMMENDED METHODOLOGY

Introduce the lesson with the question and answer method and learn the problems that students have had with intercession. Take notes of the most frequent problems that students mention (lack of perseverance, fervor, faith, etc.). Then throughout your lecture, explain each point of the lesson, using additional resources.

## STUDENTS' ASSIGNMENT

Challenge students to incorporate these fruitful prayers that they have learned into their daily prayer lives. Challenge students to implement the steps for claiming victory through prayer by tracking the results in writing so that the teacher can review them.

# APPLICATION

Throughout this week, dedicate 30 minutes each day to pray specifically for your ministry, for the church, for your family and for the most urgent needs. Write down the response that you receive from God during your prayer time.

# 2 Questionnaire for Further Study

1. What is prayer and why should we pray for?

_____

_____

_____

2. How could you improve your level of prayer?

_____

_____

_____

3. How should you pray to strengthen your ministry?

_____

_____

_____

4. Describe the prayers that are fruitful.

_____

_____

_____

5. How could you claim victory through prayer?

_____

_____

_____

6. What tools can you use to overcome the enemy?

_____

_____

_____

7. According to Revelation 12:11, how did they overcome the enemy?

_____

_____

_____

# Intercession Part 2

**3**
LESSON

## TEACHING OBJECTIVES

The student will understand that God entrusted fasting to His people not only for their health but also as a powerful spiritual weapon.

## STUDENT OBJECTIVES

1 The student will explain the relationship between fasting and prayer.

2 The student will explain the relationship between the Word of God and Prayer.

# BIBLICAL FOUNDATIONAL REFERENCE

## Joel 1:14

## CORRESPONDING BIBLICAL FOUNDATION

Psalm 35:13

1 Peter 5:6

Matthew 18:4

Ezra 8:21-23

2 Chronicles 20:2-4

Esther 4:15-17

Esther 5:3

Ephesians 3:20

Acts 1:8

Galatians 5:16-17

Romans 8:7

1 Corinthians 9:22-24

Joel 2:12-17

Psalm 33:6

Hebrews 4:12

Isaiah 55:11

Colossians 3:16

Hosea 4:6

John 5:39

Psalm 119

KEY VERSE

"For the word of God is living and active. Sharper than any doubled-edged sword, it penetrates even to dividing soul and spirit, joints and marrow; it judges the thoughts and attitudes of the heart"
**(Hebrews 4:12)**

## A. FASTING

1. God established fasting as a practice for His people.
Who abstained themselves from food in order to obtain
spiritual benefits.


- It afflicts the soul and reminds you of your need for God
(Psalm 35:13).
- It is an act of humility that affirms your position under
the hand of God (1 Peter 5:6).
- Through humility, you acquire the innocence of a child
(Matthew 18:4).

2. To seek God's favor (Ezra 8:21-23).

Ezra asked for direction for the people, his children and
his goods.

3. To seek help (2 Chronicles 20:2-4).

When three nations joined to battle against Judah,
Jehoshaphat proclaimed fasting for all of Judah. In
response to this cry came a prophecy: "You will not have
to fight this battle. Take up your positions; stand firm and
see the deliverance the LORD will give you" (2 Chronicles
20:17). Confusion then swept over these three nations,
and they destroyed themselves (2 Chronicles 20:22-24).

4. To avoid destruction (Esther 4:15-17, Esther 5:3).

In response to Haman's decree of destruction against
the Jews, Esther and her people proclaimed three days
of fasting. After they fasted and prayed to the Lord, she
went to the king and found grace before him. In fact,

he promised to give her everything that she requested. Because of this fast, mourning was replaced with joy and destruction was turned into salvation.

5. To strengthen the Spirit of God within you (Acts 1:8).

Jesus said that you would receive power and Paul added, "according to the power that works in us" (Ephesians 3:20), due to our carnal nature that dulls and inhibits our spiritual senses we can and should overcome challenges through fasting.

"Walk according to the Spirit and do not satisfy the desires of the flesh" (Galatians 5:16-17).
"The intentions of the flesh are enmity towards God" (Romans 8:7).
"He that fights abstains from all things" (1 Corinthians 9:24-27).

6. To bring revival (Joel 2:12-32).

For revival to come, people must first genuinely repent (Joel 2:12-17). Only then will the blessing come upon the whole nation (Joel 2:18-19) and result in revival (Joel 2:28-32).

# B. STUDYING THE SCRIPTURES

In intercession, fasting and studying the Word of God come together in the most powerful weapon against the enemy. Jesus overcame the adversary by confessing of the Word. For this reason we should saturate our minds and hearts with knowledge of the scriptures.

# C. THE POWER OF THE SCRIPTURES

"By the word of the LORD the heavens were made, and by the breath of His mouth all their host" (Psalm 33:6). The word breath originally means the Spirit of God. Both (Word and Spirit) created the universe.

Hebrews 4:12 the Word

- Is Alive - It is active and not monotonous. It has the capacity to give life (John 6:63).
- Is Effective - (Greek-Energues) which means it is operating or dynamic full of divine power and fulfills the purpose for which God sent it (Isaiah 55:11).
- Is Sharp - More than a double-edged sword (Greek -Makhaira), like the scalpel of a surgeon, a surgical knife (Hebrews 4:12).
- Preserves from destruction (Hosea 4:6).
- Gives testimony of Jesus (John 5:3).

Ways of using the Bible for more effective intercession.

1. Begin regular prayer times by reading the Word of God.

2. Ask God to give you a "rhema" word and apply it to your life.

3. Claim the promises in the Word for your life.

4. Saturate your mind with the Word to increase your faith.

5. Memorize key verses.

6. Worship God by confessing the Word.

7. Understand that the Word:

- It cleanses your way (Psalm 119:9).
- It gives understanding (Psalm 119:34).
- It helps us select our friends (Psalm 119:63).
- It Gives intelligence (Psalm119:104).
- It produces rejoicing (Psalm 119:116).
- It brings us life (Psalm 119:154).
- It causes us to praise (Psalm 119:171).
- It causes us to preach (Psalm 119:172).

# CONCLUSION

Fasting, the Word of God and intercession combined become a powerful and effective weapon.

# EVALUATION

Make a quiz that challenges the students to explain the relationship between fasting and prayer and the relationship between the Word of God and prayer.

# RECOMMENDED METHODOLOGY

Through skilled use of questions and answers, the teacher will learn how the students fast and use the Word of God. A lecture to explain the lesson should focus on fulfilling the goals and then helping the students apply the concepts to their personal lives.

# STUDENTS' ASSIGNMENT

As assigned in previous classes students should now adopt a discipline of fasting and bible study. They should present a written plan that outlines how they will organize their time to do this and the reasons behind their willingness to do it.

# APPLICATION

Propose a fast for a specific need this week. Find the verses that will help you claim the promise for that need and record the response received from God.

# 3 Questionnaire for further Study

1. What is fasting? _____
   _____
   _____

2. Why should you fast?
   _____
   _____
   _____

3. Why should you study the Word?
   _____
   _____
   _____

4. What is the power in the Scriptures?
   _____
   _____
   _____

5. How should I use the Word to make my intercession more effective?
   _____
   _____
   _____

6. What should I know when I use the Word?
   _____
   _____
   _____

7. If through your fasting and prayer you have achieved results, share them. If you have never done so, purpose to do so this week and share your experience. _____
   _____
   _____
   _____

# Knowing the Holy Spirit the Key to Effective Intercession

## 4
### LESSON

## TEACHING OBJECTIVE

The student will understand who the Spirit of God is. The student will understand that an individual's level of prayer depends on his or her relationship with the Holy Spirit.

## STUDENT OBJECTIVE

1 The student will explain the importance of the Holy Spirit in intercession.

2 The student will describe each aspect of intercession in which the Holy Spirit participates.

## BIBLICAL FOUNDATIONAL REFERENCE

Romans 8:26-27

### CORRESPONDING BIBLICAL FOUNDATION

Acts 15:18

John 16:7

Genesis 1:1-3

Hebrews 11:3

1 Corinthians 2:10-11

Hebrews 1:1-3

Luke 4:18-21

Matthew 12:28

Luke 4:36

Matthew 8:16

Acts 10:38

John 15:26

John 16:14-15

John 3:2

John 1:13

Deuteronomy 29:29

Romans 8:26-27

Ezekiel 36:25-27

John 7:37-39

2 Corinthians 1:21-22

Jude 1:20

KEY VERSE

"So he said to me, "This is the word of the LORD to Zerubbabel: Not by might nor by power, but by my Spirit, says the LORD Almighty"
**(Zechariah 4:6)**

## PURPOSE

The early church was so effective in its ministry because its members would not make decisions without the approval of the Holy Spirit (Acts 15:18). If today's church invites the Holy Spirit to take His proper place, we could enter into a supernatural ministry and evangelize the world in a short time. In order to develop an effective ministry of intercession, you must know yourself, know who God is and know how He can help you.

## 1. KNOWING OURSELVES

We are all spiritual people who live in temporal bodies. Through our senses we can express ourselves and have contact with the exterior world. Once we leave the body, we will continue to exist. The body will be destroyed but the spirit remains, for the spirit comes from the breath of God and is therefore imperishable. Death of the spirit means complete separation from God which leads to eternal suffering and torment.

## 2. KNOWING GOD

"In the beginning God created the heavens and the earth ..." (Genesis 1:1-3). In this passage the word God is Elohim, and in the Hebrew language this is a plural word. It shows us that the Father, the Son and the Holy Spirit make up the unity of God. They always work in mutual accord and live in perfect harmony. They made all of creation as a team. The Father designs, the Spirit conceives and the Word (Jesus) creates. Only through faith could we fathom the power of creation (Hebrews 11:3) and apply it to intercession.

## 3. THE HOLY SPIRIT IN JESUS

- The Spirit of God is the only who knows the thoughts of God (1 Corinthians 2:10-11).
- In ancient times the Spirit expressed Himself through the prophets but now He does so through Jesus Christ

(Hebrews 1:1-3).
- Jesus testified that the anointing of the Spirit was upon Him
  (Luke 4: 18-21).
- Through the Spirit of God He cast out demons
  (Matthew 12:28).
- With authority and power He cast out unclean spirits and they
  came out (Luke 4:36).
- With the Word He delivered and healed all the sick
  (Matthew 8:16).

## 4. THE HOLY SPIRIT IS A PERSON
   (ACTS 10:38)

Jesus said He would not leave us nor forsake us but would give us another Comforter that would be with us forever (John 15:26).

Because of having believed in Jesus, God gives us the great privilege of participating of His very nature allowing the Holy Spirit to come and be with us in our lives. This is called "The anointing" it is experiencing the divine presence in a permanent way.

## 5. THE HOLY SPIRIT GLORIFIES JESUS

John 16:14-15 "He will glorify me because He will take from mine and disclose it to you." The Holy Spirit has legal rights over all divine resources. He is willing to share them with those who have decided to glorify Jesus.

## 6. THE HOLY SPIRIT CAUSES US TO BE BORN AGAIN (JOHN 3:2)

Only through the Holy Spirit are we considered children of God. His work in our life allows us to be born again. When we accept Jesus, the spirit of life is conceived in us.

## 7. THE HOLY SPIRIT IS OUR GUIDE

The greatest protection to avoid falling into man made doctrines is to maintain a strong relationship with the Holy Spirit. He reveals to us the divine secrets and allows us to know future things.

## 8. THE HOLY SPIRIT REVEALS DIVINE SECRETS

"The Secret things belong to the Lord our God but the things revealed are for us and for our children forever...". The closest thing to the heart of God is the Spirit of God, who is the one who has come to live in our hearts and inspires us to continue on (Deuteronomy 29:29).

## 9. THE HOLY SPIRIT IN YOU

- The Holy Spirit increases the desire to pray (Romans 8:26).
- The Holy Spirit brings scripture to memory while you pray.
- The Holy Spirit makes us aware of the spiritual goals we ought to reach.
- The Holy Spirit makes us aware of needs that need to be met.
- The Holy Spirit will give us a burden to pray.
- The Holy Spirit will call you to prayer in moments of crisis.
- The Holy Spirit will give a special depth, power and faith to your prayer.
- He gives anointing to preach (Isaiah 61:1).
- Renews your spirit (Ezekiel 36:25-27).
- Gives strength to overcome (Zechariahs 4:6).
- Feel His presence like rivers of living water (John 7:37-39).
- Intercedes throughout your life (Romans 8:6-27).
- He is the guarantee that we are His (2 Corinthians 1:21-22).
- We should always pray with Him (Judas 20).

## CONCLUSION

The Holy Spirit longs for your prayer life to be powerful and effective.

## EVALUATION

Evaluate the relationship that your students are having with the

Holy Spirit.

During the evaluation you should keep in mind the proposed student objectives.

Give a quiz to evaluate whether or not the students understood the importance of the Holy Spirit in increasing their level of Intercession.

## RECOMMENDED METHODOLOGY

The "Seminar" hour in the School of Leaders is a time designed to minister the student in a deeper way. Take time to get to know the students more and let the Holy Spirit use you to minister to them through prayer.

## STUDENTS' ASSIGMENT

The student should evaluate his relationship with the Holy Spirit. He should desire to have a deeper relationship with Him.

# 4 Questionnaire for Further Study

1. Why is the Holy Spirit important in intercession?

_____

_____

2. Who is the Holy Spirit?_____

_____

_____

3. Who is God?_____

_____

_____

4. How did the Holy Spirit manifest himself in Jesus? _____

_____

_____

5. The Holy Spirit is a person. Please explain why._____

_____

_____

6. How should we glorify Jesus? _____

_____

_____

7. What does the Holy Spirit do in us?
a._____
b._____
c _____

8. How does the Holy Spirit move through me in intercession?

_____

_____

_____

_____

# Strengthening the Ministry Through Evangelism

5

LESSON

## TEACHER OBJECTIVE

That the student understands that evangelizing is doing spiritual warfare because God entrusted us the mission of rescuing those who are taken captive by the adversary.

## STUDENT OBJECTIVE

1 The student will define the word evangelize.

2 The student will explain what evangelism is.

3 The student will explain the signs that show that a person has been won to Christ.

4 The student will understand the worth that each soul has before God and that we should reach out to rescue them with the same compassion that Jesus did.

# BIBLICAL FOUNDATIONAL REFERENCE

## Matthew 28:19-20

### CORRESPONDING BIBLICAL FOUNDATION

2 Timothy 1:8-12

2 Timothy 2:2

2 Timothy 4:1-5

Isaiah 52

Acts 1:8

Hebrews 2:14-15

Luke 10:11

Ephesians 6:10

Romans 3:23

Romans 6:23

Ephesians 2:8

Acts 2:37-38

2 Corinthians 5:17

Matthew 26:41

Acts 26:19-20

**KEY VERSE**

"Yet when I preach the gospel, I cannot boast, for I am compelled to preach. Woe to me if I do not preach the gospel! If I preach voluntarily, I have a reward; if not voluntarily, I am simply discharging the trust committed to me. What then is my reward? Just this: that in preaching the gospel I may offer it free of charge, and so not make use of my rights in preaching it. Though I am free and belong to no man, I make myself a slave to everyone, to win as many as possible.  To the Jews I became like a Jew, to win the Jews. To those under the law I became like one under the law (though I myself am not under the law), so as to win those under the law"

**(1 Corinthians 9:16-20)**

# PURPOSE

The church must open its eyes, understand the times we live in and reach out to the lost with the same passion the apostle Paul did. He felt indebted to all people and that he had to give them the message of Jesus Christ. After Paul's spiritual eyes were opened he was able to see the truth about the spiritual life. He saw the two paths human beings could walk in with clarity, one of salvation and the other of perdition. The great majority of people were going down the wrong path. He understood that the mission God entrusted to him was what we may call "an impossible mission". Even then, he accepted the challenge and made a greater effort than the other apostles to take the Gospel to the ends of the earth. Because of this, those believers came to be known as, "those who turned the world upside down".

In the message he sent to his spiritual son Timothy he said:
"So do not be ashamed to testify about our Lord or ashamed of me his prisoner. But join with in suffering for the gospel, by the power of God, who has saved us and called us to a holy life –not because of anything we have done but because of his own purpose and grace. This grace was given us in Christ Jesus before the beginning of time. And of this gospel I was appointed a herald and an apostle and a teacher. That is why I am suffering as I am. Yet I am not ashamed, because I know whom I have believed, and am convinced that he is able to guard what I have entrusted to him for that day"
(2 Timothy 1:8-9, 11-12).

Later he said: "What you have heard me say before many witnesses entrust to reliable men who will also be qualified to teach others" (2 Timothy 2:2). He charged him emphatically to: Preach the Word; be prepared in season and out of season, be sober in all things, endure afflictions, do the work of evangelism, and to fulfill his ministry (2Timothy 4:1-5).

## A. WHAT IS EVANGELISM?
### Isaiah 52

This whole chapter has to do with the responsibility God has entrusted every believer to diligently do the work of an evangelist.

· It is a calling to intercession Vs. 1.

When Jonah was running, refusing to preach and embarked to a place far away from where God had sent him, while sleeping, a violent storm came and those on the ship feared for their lives.  Each one cried out to God for a miracle but Jonah did not even worry, as if he didn't care about those around him.  The sailors woke him up and asked:  "Why are you sleeping?  Cry out to your God, can't you see we're losing our lives?"  Jonah 1:4-14 Unbelievers motivate the believers to wake up and cry out to God because if there is no divine intervention the destruction would overtake them. Only the believers have the answer to transform the circumstances and that is through prayer.

· It is being girded with authority.  Dress your self with power:  God gave us authority (Acts 1:8).
· Jesus received power after overcoming death (Hebrews 2:14-15).
· Jesus sent us out and gave us the same power that He had (Matthew 28:18-19).
· We have authority to neutralize the kingdom of darkness through faith (Luke 10:19).
· We have responsibility to bring down the presence of God wherever we are.
· It is using the armor of God (Ephesians 6:10).
· It is projecting the type of ministry you will have.
· It is to put on the precious garments (Isaiah 52:1).

We choose the size of our ministerial garments.

- Size 12: When we have acquired our G12 team (our twelve), and God has given us the victory.
- Size 144: When we have helped our twelve acquire their own G12 teams.
- Size 1728: When we have achieved multiplication into the third generation.
- Size 20736: This is the result of networking. The net is made of various knots that are interwoven to form squares and these are the cell groups. If each one of these does its job, we will gain many souls for the kingdom of God. For this reason it is important that we concentrate on the cell group project. This is the best way to cast nets because people who are won in the cell groups are more easily consolidated. People you have trained will be the ones who multiply. Make a soul winner out of each one of them. When we learn to delegate responsibility the burden becomes much easier.

· Practicing self-deliverance. Isaiah 52:2b: Loose yourself from the chains around your neck, O captive daughter of Zion".

This captivity represents demonic oppression which is broken through deliverance. Each believer should identify through prayer, the types of bondage's that are oppressing his life and learn to perform self-deliverance. This comes as a result of spending time in intimacy with God where He will uncover the hidden work of the enemy for it to be done away with on the cross.

· Giving what we have received: Isaiah 52:3 "You were sold for nothing and without money redeemed you will be." Salvation is a gift from God. People did not have to pay to be lost. They will not pay to be saved.
· A privilege which blesses us: Isaiah 52:7 "How beautiful on the mountains are the feet of those who bring good news."
· Good news: We do not preach a message of condemnation. We need to take hope to the people so they will know that the answer to each one of their needs is in the Gospel, and Jesus is the solution to their problems.
· Announces peace: Restoration of homes, finances, health and for every area of their life. A message of peace.

· Proclaims that God reigns.
· Brings good news: **Goodness is the thing.** The message that we have is that everything will change positively for them.
· Announces salvation: **Salvation means taking them out of the** crisis in which they are and give them a word of hope.

Note: Each of us should pray for God to make us excellent communicators of the gospel. There are people who present lies as if they were great truths but there are others that expose the greatest truths as if they were lies. A good message can be ruined due to poor presentation. To proclaim the gospel we don't need many words, just an effective message. If you want to preach keep these four steps in mind.

1- Be clear
2- Be concise
3- Be precise
4- Preach with anointing


· It is a watchtower. Isaiah 52:8 "Listen! Your watchmen lift up their voices; together they shout for joy. When the Lord returns to Zion, they will see it with their own eyes." Someone who sees danger, prevents it.

· Keeping a life of holiness. Isaiah 52:11 "... purify yourselves, you who carry the vessels of the LORD." Regardless of where you are in ministry God has called you to a life of holiness.

## B. EVIDENCES THAT A PERSON HAS BEEN WON TO CHRIST.

· Conviction of Sin (Romans 3:23, 6:23)

True understanding that everyone has fallen short of the glory of God and that sin is what separates us from God and will condemn us for eternity. The conviction of sin brought by the Holy Spirit is for repentance.

· Faith in Christ (Ephesians 2:8)

Faith in Christ is effective if the person believes that only through Him can we be reconciled with God and have eternal life.

· Repentance (Acts 2:37,38)

A profound pain for having failed results in the desire to change our way of thinking.

· Change of Life (2 Corinthians 5:17)

True evidence that the person has left the old life, is that of a new behavior and the desire to grow spiritually.

· Prayer (Matthew 26:41)

Although in the beginning it's not easy, the person will begin acquiring the habit of prayer and understand it to be the means by which we communicate with God.

· Obedience (Acts 26:19,20)

That the person understands that obedience is fundamental for a life of holiness and growth.

## C. REQUIREMENTS GOD WANTS US TO MEET IN ORDER TO WIN SOULS

1.  Holiness
2.  Spirituality
3.  Humility
4.  Faith
5.  Simplicity
6.  Surrender to Christ

## APPLICATION

Set the goal to win at least 5 people for Christ in this week.

## EVALUATION

Questions:
Can a person be evangelized and yet not won for the Lord?
How do we know when a person has been won for Christ?
What comes first, a change of life then salvation, or vice versa?
How are we preparing ourselves to become soul winners?

# RECOMMENDED METHODOLOGY

The open discussion method serves best to introduce the lesson and to discuss the evidences of a person that has been won for the kingdom of God.

A project can be designed for this lesson along with the one about intercession so that the lessons can be learned in a more practical and hands-on way for increased understanding of the subject matter.

It is necessary that students have a good grasp of the concepts that were taught in this lesson and seek those qualities that God wants us to have in order to win souls.

# STUDENTS' ASSIGNMENT

Students should perform an evaluation of their own lives to see if they meet the requirements that God looks for; to be effective soul winners. This assignment can be turned in at the next class.

# 5 Questionnaire for further study

1. Define the word "Evangelism": _____
_____
_____

2. Who are evangelists and what do they do?_____
_____
_____

3. Why is evangelism a call to intercession?_____
_____
_____

4. How does evangelism invest us with authority?_____
_____
_____

5. How can evangelism take us to the ministry we desire?
_____
_____
_____

6. How can we practice the principle of deliverance through
   evangelism?_____
_____
_____

7. What blessings do we receive while we evangelize?_____
_____
_____

8. Which steps should we keep in mind to preach?
   a._____
   b._____
   c._____
   d._____

9. What are the evidences that a person has been won to Christ?

a. _____

b. _____

c. _____

d. _____

e. _____

f. _____

g. _____

10. What requirements does God look for in us in order to win souls?

_____

_____

_____

_____

# Evangelism
# Part 1

LESSON

## TEACHING OBJECTIVE

For the student to understand the key concepts to share the plan of salvation and the price that needs to be paid as a soul winner.

## STUDENT OBJECTIVE

1   The student will explain what a new believer needs to understand.

2   The student will explain what a soul winner needs to understand.

3   The student will describe the cost of being a soul winner.

# BIBLICAL FOUNDATIONAL REFERENCE

I Corinthians 9:20-23

## CORRESPONDING BIBLICAL FOUNDATION

Acts 13:1-12

Luke 11:20

John 9:3

John 1:12

Romans 3:23

Romans 6:23

I John 1:9

KEY VERSE

"Here I am! I stand at the door and knock.  If anyone hears my voice and opens the door, I will come in and eat with him, and he with me" (Revelation 3:20).

## A. HOW TO WIN SOULS
## FOR CHRIST

It is teamwork that consists of the intercession of the church, the disposition of the leaders, the direction of the Holy Spirit and the way in which we influence the new believers.

Acts 13:1-12

God is a God of seasons or times. He led the entire church into fasting and prayer to reveal to them how they should carry out the evangelistic work. They then had to choose the key people that would go on ahead breaking through in the spiritual realm and properly preparing the spiritual atmosphere for the salvation of people.

V. 2.     The Holy Spirit chooses the ones He will use for His glory.

V. 3.     The church guards them by the Spirit in prayer and gives them support.

V. 4.     The Holy Spirit sends them out.

V. 5.     Those chosen announce the Word of God wherever they go.

V. 6-11. They confronted demonic oppression as in the time when Israel was conquering Canaan and they had to confront and defeat Jericho first.

Paul and Barnabas had to confront Bar-Jesus. This represents satanic bondage where people find themselves trapped in the four walls of a stronghold.

Paul discerned and identified them as:

1. All deception.
2. All evil.
3. Enemy of all righteousness.
4. Opposition against a person's salvation.

Like the walls came tumbling down in Jericho, the apostle's words of authority broke through demonic powers saying:

a. The hand of God is against them. Jesus said He would cast out demons by the finger of God (Luke 11:20).

b. They remained blind. We should proclaim the demon's eyes to be blinded so that the people's spiritual eyes are opened (John 9:39).

c. They won't see the sun for some time. This means the demons are neutralized for a length of time. This is a time that God gives believers to go out and evangelize. The result is the conversion of the souls. Like in Jericho, the walls came down and the people were killed by the sword. When the walls come down we can put the seed of the Word of truth in their hearts.

## What is salvation?

It is a gift from God by which the human being can be saved.

- It is a work of regeneration.
- It is a miraculous work.
- It is a work of the Holy Spirit.

The soul winner should understand what his tasks are.

- Preaching: Needs to be well prepared.
- Personal preparation: Prayer, study of the Word, understanding the concepts.

- Resources: Handing out booklets, tracts or whatever the occasion demands.
- Visitation.
- Discipleship.

## B. THE PRICE PAID TO BE A WINNER OF SOULS

1. Identify with God's heart desired.
2. Lifestyle: righteous, blameless, irreproachable, to live what he preaches.
3. Prayer.
4. Take time to disciple.

## CONCLUSION

Winning souls requires not only loving them but also to be spiritualy prepared because we are witnesses and ambassadors of Christ in the world.

## APPLICATION

Plan activities in order to win more souls for Christ while keeping in mind what the main points of this lesson are.

## EVALUATION

Through a quiz or test you can evaluate the contents discussed in this lesson which should also be related to the above-mentioned indicators.

## RECOMMENDED METHODOLOGY

It is good for the teacher to take the first part of the lesson and discuss with the students the biblical foundation of each key point that a new believer and soul winner should understand.

The open discussion method is good so that the students can share what things they believe a new Christian and a soul winner should understand. The teacher can later explain the purpose of the lesson.

## STUDENTS' ASSIGNMENT

The student should write an essay about the cost of being a soul winner commenting about one's own experiences and the how he can do better job at winning souls.

# 6 Questionnaire for further study

1. Why should I win souls?_____
_____
_____

2. How could I win souls for Christ?_____
_____
_____
_____

3. Does the Church have anything to do with winning souls?
_____
_____
_____

4. How do I tear down strongholds that keep people from coming
   to Christ?_____
_____
_____
_____

5. What is salvation?_____
_____
_____
_____

6. What is the task of a soul winner?
_____
_____
_____

7. What price should I have to pay to win souls?
_____
_____
_____
_____

# Evangelism
# Part 2

## TEACHING OBJECTIVE

That the student develops the ability to evangelize effectively.

## STUDENT OBJECTIVE

1  Have the student give some practical insight for better evangelism.

2  Have the student explain how to overcome objections.

# BIBLICAL FOUNDATIONAL REFERENCE

## 2 Corinthians 6:2

### CORRESPONDING BIBLICAL FOUNDATION

Acts 13:38-41

Acts 17:30

Acts 18:9-10

Acts 19:6-10

Acts 26:16-18

John 3:16

Romans 3:23

Romans 6:23

John 1:12

Ephesians 2:8-9

Isaiah 1:18

Ecclesiastes 12:1

Proverbs 27:1

Proverbs 29:1

2 Corinthians 6:2

Joshua 24:18

1Corinthians 10-13

1 John 1-9

Isaiah 53:6

John 10:10

Revelations 20:15

**KEY VERSE**

"Therefore go and make disciples of all nations, baptizing them in the name of the Father and of the Son and of the Holy Spirit, and teaching them to obey everything I have commanded you. And surely I am with you always, to the very end of the age"
**(Matthew 28:19-20)**

# WHY EVANGELIZE?

Acts 13:38-50

Paul strives to persuade the Jews in Antioch so that they will turn their hearts to Jesus and explains certain things to them:

- The Gospel that he is preaching to them is for forgiveness of sins (V. 38).
- In Jesus, all who believe are justified (V. 39).
- Salvation is such a marvelous work that it is hard to understand.
- God entrusted us with the responsibility of taking light and salvation to the ends of the earth through evangelization (V. 47).
- The Word of God was spreading (V. 49).
- It brought joy to the disciples and infilling of the Holy Spirit (V. 50).

We should preach the message of repentance (Acts 17:30). Repentance is like when Israel crossed the Jordan to get to Canaan. It is leaving the old life to take on a new life in Christ. It is abandoning the wilderness to enter into the land that flows with milk and honey.

We have divine protection (Acts 18:9-10). The Lord wants us not to be distracted by adversity. Not to give way to fear but to speak because He will keep us from evil. God has many people to save in each city.

- Paul formed his group of twelve in Ephesus (Acts 19:6-7).
- Paul did not move until all had received the gospel (Acts 19:10).
- Paul functioned in the supernatural (Acts 19:6-7).
- Paul always went where God called him to go (Acts 23:11).
- Paul was very clear in his ministry (Acts 26:16-18).

He knew that:

· He had to open the people's spiritual eyes.
· That they should come out of darkness and into the light.
· That he had to take them out from the power of Satan and take them into the Lordship of Christ.
· That all this would take place when they received the forgiveness of sin.
· That God would make them participants of the inheritance prepared for His saints.

## HOW TO EVANGELIZE

It is very simple.  It is important to be guided by the Holy Spirit in order to obtain effective results.

Don't forget to:

· Prepare yourself daily in prayer to evangelize at any moment.
· "Break the ice."  Make a good first impression by showing a genuine interest for people's needs.
· Speak of Christ using your testimony together with biblical concepts of salvation.
· Guide them in the prayer of faith.  It is necessary that they take this important step.

### A) BREAK THE ICE

The two questions used in "Explosive Evangelism" were essential to breaking the ice.

If you were to die in this very moment, what would be the eternal destiny of your soul?  Some would probably answer "heaven".  Supposing that you get to heaven and the Father says:  "Why do you think you deserve eternal life?"  What would you respond?

Possibly some would speak of their good works. But we are not saved by works but by the grace of God.

Others have had a lot of success using the four spiritual laws:

Introduction: Everything that exists in the universe is governed by laws. All nature is subject to divine laws, and if we ignored them, we would be living in chaos. In the same way, God established laws to maintain balance in mankind, making it possible for them to live in spiritual freedom.

- Law #1: God loves you and has a wonderful plan for your life (John 3:16).
- Law #2: Man is a sinner and is separated from God. Therefore man cannot know the love of God (Romans 3:23- 6:23).
- Law #3: Jesus Christ is the only provision from God for man's sin. Only in Him can people know and experience the redemptive love of God (Romans 5:8).
- Law #4: You should accept Jesus Christ as Lord and Savior of your life in a personal way (John 1:12; Ephesians 2:8-9).

## SUGGESTIONS

- Create an atmosphere that is easy and trustworthy.
- Ask questions to build out whatever knowledge they may have of God and concerning possible religious practices.
- Be careful not to judge or cause people shame.
- Avoid giving the impression that you're a know-it-all.
- Be careful about arguments because you may win an argument but lose the opportunity for that person to be saved.
- Be very natural; avoid giving the impression that you're a religious or mystic.

### B) OBJECTIONS

Some may feel that they have insufficient biblical knowledge. Others may think that they are not worthy, etc. But when a change has occurred in the heart of the believer the Lord awakens the spirit of love and commitment for His work.

- God invites us to get right with Him (Isaiah 1:18).
- God gives us the opportunity to serve Him
  (Ecclesiastes 12:1).
- God wants us to give him all of our days (Proverbs 27:1).
- God called us to serve him willingly (Proverbs 29:1).
- Today is the day of salvation (2 Corinthians 6:2).
- All of our house should be consecrated to the service of God
  (Joshua 24:15).

## C) GENUINE OBSTACLES

- I'm afraid of not being faithful (I Corinthians 10:13).
- I fear that I have gone too far: God cannot forgive me
  (I John 1:9).
- I am not bad (Romans 3:23, Isaiah 53:6).
- I want to enjoy life (John 10:10).
- What will my friends think? (Revelations 20:15).

## C) NOT KNOWING HOW TO CRECEIVE CHRIST

Have them receive Him using the sinner's prayer.

## CONCLUSION

It is necessary to become actively involved in the work of evangelism in order to improve our skills and do a better job of evangelism.

## APPLICATION

Write a list of obstacles you have had during a time of evangelism and search for solutions in the Word.

## EVALUATION

If you are currently working on some evangelistic outreach project, this will be the best way to evaluate your students' way of evangelizing. A Quiz or short test will help measure if the students understood the lesson.

## RECOMMENDED METHODOLOGY

Students could share experiences about evangelizing and the objections they have run into. This can be the subject you share about.

## STUDENTS' ASSIGNMENT

Have your students study these points in order to complete the project.

# 7 Questionnaire for further study

1. What is the reason for evangelization according to Acts 13:38-41?

_____
_____
_____

2. How can we evangelize?

_____
_____
_____

3. What does breaking the ice mean?

_____
_____
_____

4. List at least 5 suggestions to be able to break the ice.

_____
_____
_____

5. Which are some objections we could run into when we evangelize?

_____
_____
_____

6. List the obstacles that people may have to not receive Christ.

_____
_____
_____

7. How can you lead someone in receiving Christ?

_____
_____
_____

# Evangelism
# Part 3

## LESSON 8

### TEACHING OBJECTIVE

To improve the skills necessary for evangelism through a project or through a workshop.

### STUDENT OBJECTIVE

1   The student will pray to see the Word of God in this project.

2   The student will practice what has been taught in the lessons on intercession and on Evangelism.

## BIBLICAL FOUNDATIONAL REFERENCE

John 4:1-42

### CORRESPONDING BIBLICAL FOUNDATION

Acts 21:8

Isaiah 61:1

Matthew 4:17, 23

Matthew 9:35

Matthew 26:13

Luke 24:47

Romans 15:20

1 Peter 1:12

KEY VERSE

"Preach the Word; be prepared in season and out of season; correct, rebuke and encourage with great patience and careful instruction"
**(2 Timothy 4:2)**

## Jesus and the Samaritan woman

John 4:1-42

Back then, the resentment and strife between the Jews and the Samaritans was very great. The Jews saw the Samaritans as impure because they had intermarried with the Babylonians. For this reason they would not even come close to greet them nor would they go through their cities. The Lord Jesus Christ did so because He came to tear down the wall of separation and to make both peoples into one. He also came to seek and to save that which was lost.

· Jesus broke the ice (V. 7). "Give me to drink." Jesus used a phrase that became the key to establishing a dialogue with this woman.

The woman answered that what Jesus was doing was incorrect because the custom was that they did not speak with each other.

· Jesus awoke her curiosity (V. 10). He spoke of a gift that God had for her (a gift from God) but for her to obtain it, she first was to quench His thirst and then God would quench her thirst.

The woman answered: What you are saying does not make sense.

· Jesus created a need (V. 14). Whoever has this water has resolved their problems forever.

The woman answered: I want it. Jesus led her to a point where the woman desired her salvation.

· Jesus gave her the opportunity for her family to be saved (V. 16).

The woman tries to disguise her situation.

· Jesus gives her a word of knowledge that definitely convinces her.

The woman answered: She tries to change the subject.

· Jesus guides her to true worship (V. 24).

· Jesus revealed Himself as God. "I am" (Exodus 3:14).

As a result of this conversation, the woman felt convicted and left her water jar which represented her old life and went back and won her whole city for Christ.

## CONCLUSION

It is necessary to speak in season and out of season as Jesus did; taking every opportunity that God grants us to share the love of Christ with people.

## RECOMMENDED METHODOLOGY

This lesson should be used for:

· Completing the project planned at the beginning of the course.
· Evaluating the project developed between the prior lesson and this one.
· In case the project is not carried out, this lesson should be used for a workshop about evangelism to achieve the goal of this lesson.

Plan your workshop in the way that will most benefit your class. It is important for them to know, in real life, how to break the ice with new people or how to overcome objections.  The next teaching could be used as a guide for how a workshop should be.

## APPLICATION

This week, set the goal to bring out the "evangelistic" characteristics in you, by winning at least 5 souls for Christ.

## STUDENTS' ASSIGNMENT

Find at least 3 passages in the bible where Jesus and His disciples evangelized.

# 8 Questionnaire for further study

1. Using John 4:1-12, explain how Jesus broke the ice with the Samaritan woman. _____
   _____
   _____

2. Why were the Samaritans and Jews not supposed to get along?_____
   _____
   _____

3. Jesus created a need in the Samaritan woman. How did He do it?_____
   _____
   _____

4. How did Jesus use the opportunity to touch her heart and reveal the truth?_____
   _____
   _____

5. How did Jesus guide the Samaritan woman to true worship?
   _____
   _____
   _____

6. What happened in the life of the Samaritan woman during her encounter with Jesus?_____
   _____

7. How did Jesus reveal Himself as God to the Samaritan woman?_____
   _____

8. What did the Samaritan woman do after her encounter with Jesus?_____
   _____
   _____

# Serving Others
# Part 1

LESSON

## TEACHING OBJECTIVE

That the student would understand what serving others is and biblical examples of its importance in the ministry.

## STUDENT OBJECTIVE

1   The student is to define service.

2   The student is to give two examples of people that were role models in serving others.

# BIBLICAL FOUNDATIONAL REFERENCE

## John 13:1-16

### CORRESPONDING BIBLICAL FOUNDATION

Deuteronomy 6:13

Joshua 24:15

Psalm 100:2

Malachi 3:18

Matthew 4:10

Matthew 6:24

Luke 4:39

John 12:26

Acts 20:19

KEY VERSE

"For even the Son of Man did not come to be served, but to serve, and to give his life as a ransom for many"
**(Mark 10:45)**

The principle of service comes directly from the life of the Lord Jesus who decided voluntarily to leave His throne of Glory where all the angels served and adored Him, to serve His church. If men could understand this principle, they would treat their wives better, parents would do the same with their children, leaders with their disciples and the pastors with their flock.

I know that some of those who begin in ministry desire the supernatural and for the power of God to be manifested through them. But the Lord always looks at the attitude of the heart and entrusts us with simpler responsibilities to mold our character and test the measure our faithfulness. If we are faithful in the little, He will be able to entrust us with more.

## A. WHAT IS TO SERVE?

· It is an internal attitude that shows its fruit in the external actions (Matthew 24:45-46).
· It is being useful (Luke 17:7-10).
· It is a fundamental characteristic in a disciple of Christ (Matthew 23:11-12).
· It is unconditional. It expects nothing in return (John 5:17).
· It is a determination that we take on (I Corinthians 9:27).
· It motivates people to glorify God (2 Corinthians 9:13).
· It is a work of love (Galatians 5:13, Ephesians 2:10).

## B. EXAMPLES

· God honored Joshua because He had served Moses (Joshua 1:1).
· Elijah was the authority over Elisha and for his

faithfulness he received a double anointing
(2 kings 2:1-3).

· Jesus demonstrated his service offering His life for
the redemption of many (Matthew 20:28).

· After the first servants were anointed for this work a
great revival came to the church (Acts 6:5,8).

· Paul makes the decision to serve in order to gain the
greatest possible number of people
(I Corinthians 9:19).

Explain how they were serving and how God used each one of
them.

## CONCLUSION

You can only become a servant, serving others.

## APPLICATION

Record at least two daily acts of service and write down your
experience.

## EVALUATION

The definition of service could easily be evaluated in a quiz. In the
final exam, you will need to take the above mentioned students'
objectives into account.

## RECOMMENDED METHODOLOGY

Lecturing could be used to define what serving is. Then, to unfold
examples of service, divide the students into groups and assign
a person, from the bible to be studied. Present the complete
research to the class.

## STUDENTS' ASSIGNMENT

Students should describe the areas in which the attitude of service could be developed explaining how it will be done.

# 9 Questionnaire for further study

1. Explain the meaning of what it is to serve.

_____

_____

_____

_____

_____

2. What does serving imply?

_____

_____

_____

_____

_____

3. List at least three examples of service in the Bible.

_____

_____

_____

_____

_____

4. Define the word servant._____

_____

_____

_____

_____

5. Mention at least 5 servants of God and what they did for others._____

_____

_____

_____

6. How are we to do acts of service for God and for others?

_____

_____

_____

_____

_____

7. Which acts of service did Jesus perform?  Describe at least
   three using with the corresponding biblical citations.

_____

_____

_____

_____

# Serving Others
# Part 2

10
LESSON

## TEACHING OBJECTIVE

That the student understands the importance of
serving others in the ministry by looking at Steven's
life.

## STUDENT OBJECTIVE

1   The student will explain who Steven was and the
    importance of his ministry in the early church.

2   The student will specifically define the characteristics
    of a great ministry.

BIBLICAL FOUNDATIONAL
REFERENCE

Acts 6:1-10

CORRESPONDING
BIBLICAL
FOUNDATION

Acts 20:19

Romans 9:12

Romans 12:7

1 Corinthians 9:13

Galatians 5:13

Colossians 3:24

KEY VERSE

"Not so with you. Instead,
whoever wants to become
great among you must be
your servant"
**(Matthew 20:26)**

## SERVICE

Is what characterizes great ministries and it is the example that a true servant of God shows.

## A. STEPHEN, A TRUE EXAMPLE

Acts 6:1-10

V. 8.   He was full of grace and power.  God honored him with signs among the people.

V. 9.   His adversaries could not resist the wisdom or the Spirit with which Stephen spoke.

V. 15.  His face was like that of an Angel.

V. 14.  The secret of his ministry was service

Although he was not counted among the apostles he was able to develop the work of service with the same passion that the apostles did.

V. 3.   The three requirements of the servants were:

- They should be people of a good testimony.

- Filled with the Holy Spirit.

- Filled with wisdom.

Do explain these three concepts to the students.

# B. CHARACTERISTICS OF SERVICE AND OF SERVANTS OF GOD

a. Having a servant's heart.

- Using our talents to serve God (Ephesians 4:11-13).
- Being patient in adversity (Colossians 1:24).
- Consecrating our lives completely to the service of God (2 Timothy 2:1-4).
- For our mutual edification (1 Peter 2:4).
- Giving ourselves tirelessly to people (I Thessalonians 2:9).

b. Mistaken arguments with regards to service.

- Some believe that: It is a dishonorable attitude.
- Those who do not have a ministry are the ones who should serve.
- That it is done to gain favor with the leaders.
- That it is related to the wearing of certain types of clothing.

c. Service gives greatness.

- It is a requirement, not an option.
- Jesus commanded men to serve their wives as He did with His church (Ephesians 5:25).
- Jesus said that he who humbles himself as a child will be great in the kingdom of God (Matthew 18:4).

## CONCLUSION

Like Stephen, God also wants to use us but we should tear down arguments in our minds so that we understand that the key to great ministries is serving others.

## APPLICATION

Ask your leader to assign you a task to perform during the Sunday service. Then write down your experiences and share them with two other persons.

# EVALUATION

In the final exam, you can see if the student has understood the importance of service in the ministry.

## RECOMMENDED METHODOLOGY

The lecture method may be used to explain the lesson. An exhaustive analysis of Stephen's life is important to the goal of this lesson. Use a study Bible in order to achieve that.

## STUDENTS' ASSIGNMENT

The students should establish principles in their lives in reference to service in ministry.

# 10 Questionnaire for further study

1. Explain the basic characteristic of great ministries.

_____

_____

_____

2. Who was Stephen?_____

_____

_____

_____

3. What were his characteristics?_____

_____

_____

_____

4. Which are the requirements of a servant?

_____

_____

_____

_____

5. How could we have a servant's heart?_____

_____

_____

_____

6. Which arguments or objections do people use against service?

_____

_____

_____

_____

7. What happens when we became servants?_____

_____

_____

_____

# BIBLIOGRAPHIES

- The Personal Evangelism. Myer Pearlman.

- Spiritual Reproduction.  James D. Crane. Baptist
  House of Publications

- Born to Multiply. Dawson Trotman.

- Winners of Men.  Charles Spurgeon.

- Encounter. Cesar Castellanos

- A Challenge to Serve. Charles R. Swindoll.

- Where to find it in the Bible. Ken Anderson.

- New Illustrated Bible Dictionary.